ELUCIDATIONS

ALSO BY PARKER BONO

THE STANCE TO LEAD

THE STANCE TO GET ELECTED

THE TRUTH ABOUT THE FED

LIBERALISM DEBUNKED

*As always,
I dedicate this book to the American people
and those who fight and fought for me and
my rights.*

Contents

CHAPTER ONE

TAXATION

"There comes a time when one must take a position
that is neither safe, nor politic, nor popular, but he
must take it because conscience tells him it is right."
-Martin Luther King Jr.

Our current tax code is more than 5 times larger, in
terms of words, than the bible. It is far too
complicated and it needs to be changed. On
taxation, there is little room for one to compromise.
I would like the tax code to be 25 words, while
some are totally fine with our current tax code. If
we were to meet in the middle, we still have
approximately 2 million words.

A truly great tax plan is yet to be introduced. All of
the tax plans proposed would still create a very
large cost of compliance. These plans still have very
confusing deductions, are eligible to any American,
have fairly high, as well as unfair, tax rates, and
most importantly, they add to the deficit, with no
plan to offset costs. Some of the proposed plans will
indeed help us economically, but not as much as
they could be, and that is perhaps the largest
problem we are facing right now: America, as well
as many of its citizens, have given up on even so
much as attempting to reach their full potential. If

we were willing to restore prosperity and strive for reformation that improves our country, particularly on taxation, we would be taking monumental steps towards excellence.

To begin the reformation of the immensely complex tax code, we must first address personal income tax rates. The cost of compliance for personal income taxes alone is $100 billion annually. This means that, due to complications in the tax code, Americans waste over 2.6 billion hours each year filing their taxes, which equates to about $100 billion in lost potential GDP, and therefore a loss in revenue. The tax code obviously needs to be simplified.

The solution to the problem is a two bracket tax system, with absolutely no deductions available. The first bracket would be at 0%, and one would fall into this bracket if they made less than $88,100 annually. That's right: if you make less than $88,100 annually, you would pay no taxes to the federal government, with the exception of FICA, or payroll taxes. This plan would save the average household about $5,000 annually. The next bracket would be at 15%, and one would fall into this bracket if they made over $88,100 annually. This would save each individual in this bracket money each year. Under this plan, everyone gets a tax cut, but that's not all. GDP would also increase very close to $100 billion due to the fact there will be essentially no more cost of compliance.

Finally, revenue would increase $88 billion annually due to this part of the plan alone. Just as witnessed when President Kennedy and President Reagan lowered tax rates, revenue will increase as a result, due to the laffer curve. President Kennedy lowered the top personal tax rate from 90% to 70%, and the result was $94 billion in increased revenues. President Reagan lowered tax rates at every bracket, almost as proposed above, and the result was yet again a revenue increase, this time of 99.4%, throughout the 1980's.

Finally, this federal income tax plan would increase GDP by approximately 2%, annually. This is merely from the change to the individual tax rates. This is yet another reason for individual income tax cuts, but more specifically, this proposition.

After tackling personal income taxation, it is time to move on to corporate income taxation. The United States has the 3rd highest corporate income tax rates in the world, and the absolute highest when compared to all other developed countries. To encourage economic growth, this tax must be reformed. Corporate income taxes absolutely can not be raised, as doing so will cause great economic damage.

Lowering the corporate income tax rate certainly will help the economy, but if America's full economic potential is to be reached, the corporate income tax must be eliminated, entirely.

The first of many reasons the corporate income tax should be eliminated is due to the fact that the tax isn't paid by the corporation. The tax revenue is taken out of your pocket. According to the *CBO,* or Congressional Budget Office, 30% of the tax is paid by workers, while 70% is paid by shareholders. This means that both investors and workers are losing a tremendous sum of money.

This appends to the second point, which is that eliminating the corporate income tax will increase wages. According to *The Tax Foundation,* real wages would increase around 2% if the corporate income tax is eliminated, entirely. However, according to the *Tax Analysis Center*, eliminating the corporate income tax will increase real wages by 12%, on average. The case the *Tax Analysis Center* made was strong enough for *The New York Times* to write an op-ed on the findings. Even if corporations only increased the salaries of executives (they wouldn't), tax revenue would still increase, by reason of the new income still being taxed at the federal level.

This increase in income will result in the substantial GDP growth , which is the third reason to eliminate the corporate income tax. The current corporate income tax is resulting in a tremendous loss of potential economic growth. This is for a number of reasons. Firstly, according to *The Tax Foundation,* eliminating the corporate income tax would result in a 2% increase in GDP. This means that the current corporate income tax is stalling GDP growth by approximately 2%. Additionally, an increase in either investment or spending will occur when salaries of both individuals, as well as corporations, are accelerated. This adds on the fourth reason to abolish the corporate income tax.

The fourth reason to abolish the corporate income tax is because doing so will result in great financial gains and economic prosperity. The stock market is forecasted to increase 17% almost immediately after the elimination of the corporate income tax. This is a substantial increase. The average American owns approximately $12,000 in stocks, according to the Federal Reserve. This means that a 17% increase of stocks would increase the value of the average American's portfolio by over $2,000. However, it gets even better for grandma and grandpa. The average 401(k) has an estimated value of approximately $96,495, according to *Vanguard's "How America Saves"* report. This means that the average 401(k)'s value will increase by over $16,000 almost immediately after the corporate income tax is ended.

On a static estimate, the impact eliminating the corporate income tax has on the federal budget is a loss of approximately $340 billion. However, this estimate does not take into account the growth in revenue from the resulting economic growth. A dynamic estimate does. On a dynamic estimate, the impact eliminating the corporate income tax has on the federal budget is a loss of approximately $300 billion. However, unlike other tax plans, this plan has methods to offset the losses, as well as create net gains in revenue. This loss of $300 billion in revenue brings the net loss of revenue in this tax plan up to $212 billion when also accounting for the personal income tax plan, which raises revenue by $88 billion.

By abolishing the corporate income tax, we as a nation will be reaching our full economic potential, grandma and grandpa would be living an exponentially better life in retirement, the average American's salary will increase, GDP would grow faster than witnessed in recent history, more jobs will be created, and the U.S. will be leading the world once again.

After fixing the corporate income tax, it is time to deal with the loss in revenue. This must be achieved via new taxation.

Firstly, the United States must begin to tax added sugar consumption. The United States has an obesity epidemic. We are the 12th most obese country in the world. The main reason for this is a poor diet, particularly in added sugar. If the United States were to tax all added sugar at $0.02, or one penny, per gram, approximately $470 billion would be raised, assuming Americans consumed sugar at the same rate, which would mean the increased cost did not deter Americans from their habits. This tax is a win regardless of the result. If the tax generated $0, no added sugar would be consumed across all of America, which means that the health of Americans would improve exponentially. However, if the tax does not stop Americans from eating approximately 160 pounds of added sugar annually, the government will collect over $470 billion. This $470 billion creates a net gain in revenue of $258 billion in this tax plan. Some of this revenue should go towards anti-sugar campaigns.

Next, marijuana should be legalized across the nation, and taxed at a 25% rate. The war on drugs has failed. It has cost over $1 trillion and has ultimately decreased illegal drug prices, and therefore increased illegal drug use. It is hard enough to attempt to terminate the distribution of illicit drugs, and even harder, and more intrusive, to attempt to terminate the growth of a plant.

Legalizing marijuana would put many drug lords out of business, as well as ensure that non-pure marijuana stays out of the market. This will decrease the amount of deaths caused by dangerous and fake drugs. It is not a smart choice to decide to smoke marijuana, especially if you are below the age of 21. However, if you are an adult and decide to smoke marijuana, as moronic as you are, and as useless as doing so is, it is not the government's right to stop you, so long as you are not causing harm to anyone else.

However, the legalization of marijuana should not make one feel as though they will be able to smoke marijuana and collect welfare. One still must pass a drug test to collect welfare, for the reasons that people had to take a drug test to be hired to a position in which they eventually funded your welfare payments, as well as the fact that allowing a society to be lazy potheads and collect money does absolutely nothing but harm to society. Society can function if immoral things exist. However, society cannot function if immoral things are classified as moral.

Finally, legalizing marijuana and taxing all sales at a 25% rate will generate approximately $12.5 billion annually. A portion of this revenue should go towards anti-drug campaigns among teens and anti-drug campaigns in the inner cities, as well as anti-opioid campaigns. This $12.5 billion brings the net gain of revenue in this tax plan up to approximately $270.5 billion.

Additionally, online gambling should be legalized nationwide, and all deposits should be taxed at a 10% rate. There is no reason not to allow online gambling, just like there is no reason for the federal government to regulate state lotteries. If one would like to risk their money, whether it be on stocks or on a deck of cards, why should the federal government care? Taxing all online gambling deposits will generate approximately $2.5 billion annually. This $2.5 billion brings the net gain of revenue in this tax plan up to $273 billion.

Next, a federal sales tax must be implemented. This tax should stand at 1%. This tax will be implemented upon the sale of any item. Almost every state and local government has this kind of tax. Additionally, this federal sales tax would encourage one to save or invest more than spend, which is preferable to a growing economy. If the federal government implemented this 1% sales tax, about $27 billion in revenue would be generated. This brings the net gain in revenue of this tax plan up to $300 billion.

Additionally, there are multiple already instated taxes that must be totally eliminated. The first of these taxes is referred to as the gas tax. The current federal gas tax rate stands at 18.4 cents per gallon. However, this is in addition to the average of 31.04 cents per gallon charged by states. This is the average, but in states such as New York, Hawaii, Washington, and Pennsylvania, one pays over 60 cents per gallon to the state and federal government.

Overall, the average price of gas per gallon in the U.S. is approximately $2.56. This means that eliminating the federal gas tax alone will result in an average reduction in gas prices of 7%. It is possible, and even probable, that the price of gas will go up again over time, but the price will no longer be artificially altered in any way by the federal government.

Driving in a car that you paid for, with renewed registration that you paid for, as well as a renewed driver's license that you paid for, is not bad for you, unlike consuming 160 pounds of sugar annually. The federal government should not intervene in the free market by taxing gas prices in yet another attempt to increase the cost to go from point A to point B in the most efficient way possible. To the contrary, the government should care about the health of its citizens, which is why sugar must be taxed. The current revenue of the gas tax goes towards infrastructure, just like some of the revenue from the cigarette tax goes towards anti-cigarette campaigns. However, in the case of the gas tax, we are taxing the wrong commodity. Nobody is arguing that the U.S. should decrease infrastructure spending. However, the items being taxed to fund infrastructure projects should be changed. The effect ending the federal gas tax has on this tax plan is a loss of approximately $40 billion in revenue, bringing the net gain of this tax plan down to about $260 billion.

The final existing tax that must end is known as the estate and gift tax. This tax is also referred to as the "death tax". This tax is a 40% tax on assets passed on to heirs that amount to $5.5 million, or more. There are so many issues with this tax, the first of which being that the federal government has no right to deem what amount of money is too much. Nobody has the right to tell someone that there is a point to which they can no longer rise to. Even if they are Bill Gates, one has no right to tell them they have too much money.

The next issue with the estate and gift tax is the minimum amount of wealth required for this tax to be applicable. $5.5 million dollars is not chump change, but it certainly does not make you very rich. Approximately 928,000 households in the U.S. have a net worth of over $5,000,000. The estate tax caps the point to which you should grow, so any estate tax is wrong. However, the tax would be arguable if it did not effect over 928,000 households in a drastically negative way. Those who are the most affected by the current estate and gift tax are small businessmen. They are not the fat cats that you think they are. These small businessmen work extremely hard to create wealth, as well as attempt to create a better future for their heirs. However, just because grandpa has a heart attack, his $6 million in assets would immediately turn into $3.6 million. This is not a laughable figure to families, but it is a laughable figure to the federal government. The $2.4 million in revenue the federal government would receive would fund the federal government for about 21 seconds. However, that extra $2.4 million could change the lives of that family, and, if used efficiently to create jobs, the lives of many more families.

Additionally, the estate and gift tax imposes multiple burdens upon the U.S. economy. Eliminating the estate tax will create approximately 31,250 jobs annually, increase GDP by approximately $10 billion annually, increase capital stock value by about $80 billion annually, and increase personal income by about $8 billion annually. The economic effects of eliminating the estate and gift tax far outweigh the small amount of revenue created by the tax. The estate and gift tax raises enough revenue to fund the federal government for slightly more than two days, or about 55 hours. This is equivalent to about 0.15% of the U.S. GDP in 2016.

The idea that wealth is merely handed to most billionaires is wrong. Only one of the Americans in the top 25 on the *Forbes* list inherited their wealth (the Walton family). All of the others, including Bill Gates, Warren Buffett, Michael Bloomberg, and Michael Dell, earned their wealth by taking risks and via innovation. Success is not exclusively available to currently successful families. Anybody can become the next Bill Gates.

The effect eliminating the estate and gift tax has on federal revenue is a loss of approximately $23 billion. This loss brings the net gain of this tax plan down to about $237 billion. However, there are multiple economic benefits that result from the elimination of the estate and gift tax.

Finally, the last currently implemented tax that must be eliminated is the federal cigarette tax. The cigarette tax does not deter people from smoking. If the cigarette tax is designed to stop people from smoking, then what is the personal income tax designed to do? When one is addicted to a product, they will do anything they can to acquire that product. This includes skipping meals, as witnessed when states increase the cigarette tax rate per pack.

Most smokers are low income earners, so they spend a much higher percentage of their income on cigarettes. For example, in New York, this percentage is 23.6%. However, since 23.6% of one's income was just spend on cigarettes, they now lack the funds necessary to obtain food. This leaves low income earners either skipping meals or applying for food stamps from the federal government. This means that because a state increased the cigarette tax, the federal government must increase spending. This effect causes a revenue transfer, and wipes out the revenue obtained.

Nobody is encouraging smoking, smoking is a very bad habit, and the government should care about the health of its citizens, which is why sugar should be taxed. However, the sugar tax is yet to be attempted, so it is unknown whether or not it will deter Americans from eating 160 pounds of sugar annually. If it does, America's health improves. If the tax does not deter Americans from consuming

160 pounds of sugar annually, the federal government collects hundreds of billions of dollars as a result of the bad habits. However, unless the U.S. increases the amount of money allotted for food stamps, those who are on food stamps will be forced to consume less sugar, because they will be unable to afford as much sugar.

To the contrary, the cigarette tax causes the federal government to spend more by reason of smokers having less money. This problem could be partially fixed by reforming the welfare system, but the problem could be entirely fixed by eliminating the federal cigarette tax, and reforming the welfare system. This would mean that the federal cigarette tax would no longer decrease revenue received by states by $2.3 billion annually, and by reforming the welfare system, the state cigarette tax will no longer cost the federal government as much each fiscal year.

The effect eliminating the federal cigarette tax has on revenue is a loss of approximately $15 billion. However, the $15 billion will be essentially gained back by reforming the welfare system, but this will only be taken into account later. This loss of $15 billion brings the net gain of this tax plan down to $245 billion annually.

Finally, the only already implemented tax that must increase is the custom duty. This is a tax on all items that are sent from other countries to the

United States. All of these duties should be doubled. This means that if no corporate income tax, as well as a lower personal income tax on profits is not enough to bring some of the companies here, they will pay for this decision. Additionally, this will help the United States become independent and once again be the exceptional leader of the world. The effect doubling all custom duties has on federal revenue is an increase of about $35 billion. This brings the net gain of this tax plan up to $280 billion.

In conclusion, this tax plan would increase GDP by at least 4% annually, create millions of jobs, increase wages by at least an additional 2% annually, improve the health of Americans, save Americans thousands of dollars annually, increase the value of the stock market by around 17% almost immediately after the implementation of this tax plan, and create a net revenue gain of $280 billion.

CHAPTER TWO
GUNS

"Laws that forbid the carrying of arms...disarm only those who are neither inclined nor determined to commit crimes. Such laws make things worse for the assaulted and better for the assailants; they serve rather to encourage than prevent homicides, for an unarmed man may be attacked with greater confidence than an armed one."
-Thomas Jefferson

The second amendment to the U.S. Constitution is one of the most important amendments. According to the Supreme Court case *District of Columbia v. Heller*, "The Second Amendment protects an individual right to possess a firearm unconnected with service in a militia, and to use that arm for traditionally lawful purposes, such as self-defense within the home." This decision is astronomical: liberals became stumped.

Not only is there a Supreme Court decision in favor of the second amendment, but the words are also clearly written into the second amendment of the U.S. Constitution. The second amendment states "A well regulated Militia, being necessary to the security of a free State, the right of the people to keep and bear Arms, shall not be infringed." Adversary's of the second amendment tend to argue two points: the phrase "well regulated militia" proves that the second amendment is antiquated, and the second amendment only referred to muskets at the time in which it was written.

The first point adversary's of the second amendment use is easily debunked by looking at practically anything written during the time era in which the U.S. Constitution was written. Instead, opponents of the second amendment tend to read *The Washington Post*, *Salon*, *Rolling Stone*, and *CNN*. All of the media organizations above have either themselves advocated for the repeal of the second amendment or have given a platform to those that possess such a view.

The following examples are just a few of the many that disprove the adversary's first argument, and all of which are taken from the *Oxford English Dictionary*. "If a liberal Education has formed in us well-regulated Appetites and worthy Inclinations." (1709), "The practice of all well-regulated courts of justice in the world." (1714), "The equation of time … is the adjustment of the difference of time as shown by a well-regulated clock and a true sundial." (1812), "A remissness for which I am sure every well-regulated person will blame the Mayor." (1848), "It appeared to her well-regulated mind, like a clandestine proceeding." (1862), and "The newspaper, a never wanting adjunct to every well-regulated American embryo city." (1894). Each and every one of these quotes prove that the term "well-regulated" was commonly used in the century preceding, as well as the century after, the second amendment was written. These quotes also manifest that the term "well-regulated" meant "properly functioning" or "trained/disciplined" during the time period in which the second amendment was written.

Additionally, the word "militia" also had divergent meanings during the time period in which the second amendment was written. According to 10 U.S. Code § 246, a militia is defined as so: "The militia of the United States consists of all able-bodied males at least 17 years of age and, except as provided in section 313 of title 32, under 45 years of age who are, or who have made a declaration of intention to become, citizens of the United States and of female citizens of the United States who are members of the National Guard." Remember, this is still an existing U.S. Code, meaning this is current federal law. Additionally, U.S. Codes are permanent. The rest of 10 U.S. Code § 246 is written as so: "The classes of the militia are

> (1) the organized militia, which consists of the National Guard and the Naval Militia; and
> (2) the unorganized militia, which consists of the members of the militia who are not members of the National Guard or the Naval Militia."

In all, this current U.S. Code, or federal law, states that the definition of the term "militia" is all able-bodied American men aged between 17 and 45, as well as all women in the National Guard or Naval Militia. This militia does not need to be organized either, since the second class militia is defined as all pupils who fit the above requirements, and who are not members of the National Guard or Naval Militia.

If additional proof is required for one to believe this claim, perhaps a quote from the co-author of the second amendment will be convincing enough. "I ask, Sir, what is the militia? It is the whole people. To disarm the people is the best and most effectual way to enslave them." This quote is from George Mason, the co-author of the second amendment, and was documented during Virginia's Convention to Ratify the Constitution in 1788.

The second point adversary's of the second amendment make can also be easily debunked by looking at another history book. The second amendment absolutely did not only refer to muskets only. One who assumes this is assuming that the founding fathers were so ignorant that they anticipated no innovation whatsoever in weaponry. However, the founding fathers did more than anticipate innovation: they witnessed innovation.

The first of the multiple weapons that were similar to current "assault weapons" was called a girandoni air rifle. This gun had the ability to fire approximately 22 rounds per minute, without requiring a single reload. This was at least 7 times the rate of fire of a musket, supposedly the only gun that existed in the 1700's, according to liberals.

Additionally, President Thomas Jefferson sent Lewis and Clark with this very gun on their expedition.

However, the girandoni air rifle is not the only gun that is similar to current "assault weapons." Another one of such guns was known as the belton flintlock. The belton flintlock shot approximately 8 rounds in the pull of one trigger. This gun worked essentially like a roman candle: after the fuse is lit, merely pull the trigger once, then aim the shots that will automatically come out thereafter. To quote Joseph Belton, the inventor of the gun, "May it Please your Honours, I would just informe this Honourable Assembly, that I have discover'd an improvement, in the use of Small Armes, wherein a common small arm, may be maid to discharge eight balls one after another, in eight, five or three seconds of time." Eight shots in approximately 3 seconds is a very rapid rate of fire. However, the founding fathers did not regulate this gun in any way whatsoever.

Additionally, another gun that was similar to current "assault weapons" was called a 24 barrel pepperbox revolver. This revolver is fairly self explanatory: the gun held 24 rounds, and shot them as fast as one could pull the trigger. This gun's origins can be traced back to the 1500's, so therefore the founding fathers certainly were informed of the guns' existence at the time in which the second amendment was written.

The original intent of the Second Amendment is immensely clear. Those who argue inversely are simply incorrect, and can not embrace such a fact.

Finally, there are a plethora of disinformation campaigns associated with gun related statistics within the United States. An array of legislators have made absolute ignoramuses of themselves by stating the following. "I actually do not know what a barrel shroud is (barrel shroud regulation was within proposed legislation)" -Carolyn McCarthy, 2007, "Some of these bullets, as you saw, have an incendiary device on the tip of it, which is a heat seeking device. So, you don't shoot deer with a bullet that size, if you do, you could cook it at the same time." -Patricia Eddington, 2005, "This is a ghost gun. This right here has the ability with a 30-caliber clip to disperse with 30 bullets within half a second. 30 magazine clip within half a second." -Kevin de León, 2014. The fact that individuals who lack the mental capacity to comprehend basic information pertaining to guns get to legislate such guns as they please is appalling. However, just in case you didn't know, Patricia, bullets do not have heat-seeking devices located on them. Additionally, Kevin, semi-automatic guns are not capable of shooting 30 rounds in half a second. Machine guns with multiple magazines can barely reach that level, and last time I checked, the Firearm Owners Protection Act of 1986, which banned machine guns, is still valid.

Additionally, a group of a highly selective and elite individuals are the main and practically sole contributors towards many gun control organizations. These include, but are not limited to, Michael Bloomberg, Bill Gates, Warren Buffet, Oprah, Paul Allen, Steve Ballmer, Rupert Murdoch, and the notorious George Soros, who may be indirectly linked to the evil death of countless Jews, on the basis of their religion. The following is an excerpt of an interview with George Soros, the same billionaire who funds gun control organizations across the nation. Kroft: It is my understanding that you went out with this protector of yours who swore that you were his adopted godson. Soros: Yes, Yes. Kroft: Went out, in fact, and helped in the confiscation of property from the jews. Soros: That's Right. Kroft: That sounds like an experience that would send lots of people to the psychiatric coach for many, many years. Was it difficult? Soros: Not at all. Not at all. Maybe as a child you don't see the connection, but it created no problem at all. Kroft: No feeling of guilt? Soros: No. Remember this the nest time that the media calls you a conspiracy theorist for even invoking George Soros's name. Perhaps the media is tempered by a mention of George Soros's name due to the fact that he has ties to many mainstream media outlets, but I digress.

On guns, there is little to no compromises that can be made. Gun rights are very clearly written into current law, and the agendas of gun control advocates are also very clear: to ensure that those laws change.

CHAPTER THREE
ENERGY

"I would like for nuclear fusion to become a practical power source. It would provide an inexhaustible supply of energy, without pollution or global warming."
-Stephen Hawking

In reference to energy, there are a great deal of statements to be made. The first of which is one that many will likely agree with, which is the fact that our current energy system needs reformation. The system needs to be reformed, in order to become more cost efficient, as well as environmentally efficient. Whether liberal or conservative, one must admit that it is better to use alternative energy sources as opposed to fossil fuels. The only people in disagreement are the arab nations that take advantage of our ignorance each and every second of each day, as well as oil companies. If our current energy system is to be reformed for the better, it will require a transformation.

This transformation will require investments in nuclear, hydro, solar, and wind energy. Nuclear energy should be the source most relied upon, as it is currently the most reliable of the four, most sustainable of the four, and cheapest of the four, per kilowatt hour, with hydropower the only source remotely close in any of the categories.

Nuclear energy is an extremely underrated power source. It's very rare, but often catastrophic, disasters lead many to believe that the power source as a whole is dangerous. However, this is far from the case. Nuclear energy is actually the safest source of energy production. When looking at deaths per terawatt hour, brown coal ranks highest, at 32.72, with conventional coal in second at 24.62 deaths per terawatt hour. Oil comes in third at 18.43 deaths per terawatt hour, with biomass coming in fourth at 4.63 deaths per terawatt hour, and gas coming in second to last at 2.82 deaths per terawatt hour. Nuclear energy, the safest form of energy based upon this metric, has a mere 0.07 deaths per terawatt hour rate. This makes nuclear energy over 450 times safer than brown coal, and exponentially safer than all other sources as well.

Perhaps this is just a misleading statistic, or a statistical outsider. So, let's examine the amount of carbon emitted per kilowatt hour. Coal releases the most, at 1,001 grams. Oil releases the second most, at 840 grams. Gas releases the third at 469 grams. Solar is next at 46 grams. Then comes nuclear at 16 grams. Wind and hydropower follow at 12 grams and 4 grams, respectively. In this aspect, nuclear energy does not rank first, but it is still exceptionally better than conventional energy sources, and releases three times less carbon than solar.

Finally, nuclear energy saves lives. With lower death per kilowatt hour rates, depending on which source nuclear energy replaces, anywhere from 400,000 to 7,000,000 lives could be saved by the middle of this century alone. As with everything, it is best to not follow hysteria. It is not common knowledge, but the largest nuclear accident in the history of the United States, the one that occurred at Three Mile Island in 1979, actually did not result in a single death or injury. As is such with multiple other sectors, the U.S. ranks at the top of the world in nuclear energy safety.

Conventional energy methods of coal, oil, and natural gas should be phased out, at least in the U.S. There however is good news for coal and oil companies, which will come later. The 100% alternative energy grid should consist of about 65% nuclear power, 10% hydro power, 12.5% solar power, and 12.5% wind power. This is a very balanced system, with a clean, safe, and cheap energy source as the dependable energy source (nuclear energy).

If all installations were to be fully funded within ten years, this would cost about $1 trillion, in total, or about $100 billion per year. For reference, over $1 trillion was spent on the Iraq war, which lasted less than eight years, and gave us absolutely nothing in return. We could have made 100% of our nation's energy sources alternative and reliable with the same budget.

Regardless, the cost is extremely capable to be funded, likely by federal and state cooperation. However, eliminating the use of fossil fuels within the U.S. does not eliminate the tremendous amount of fossil fuels that our nation has been blessed with. These fossil fuels may have no use in future America, but they definitely have use in other nations, across the world, especially in nations currently struggling exceedingly to succeed.

The U.S. is the largest natural gas producer in the world, and has the largest coal and oil reserves in the world. As a matter of fact, many of these untapped fossil fuels reside upon federal land, meaning the government must do nothing except sell access to such land. There are currently 55 billion barrels of natural gas on federal land, 81 billion tons of coal, and 70 billion barrels of oil. The natural gas alone is worth about $1.5 trillion, with the coal being worth an additional $3.3 trillion, and the oil being worth an additional $4.9 trillion. This totals about $9.7 trillion.

If the government were to allow companies to extract all fossil fuel on federal land, and take a flat fee of 15% on the sale of fossil fuels extracted from federal lands, over $1.4 trillion would be generated. This more than funds the alternative energy project. The fossil fuels should be extracted within ten years.

This plan benefits every party involved. The fossil fuel companies will generate over $8.2 trillion in sales, the U.S. economy as GDP would increase trillions, the fossil fuel employees as more individuals will likely be employed, as well as the fact that pay increases are almost certain, the government will receive over $1.4 trillion, the citizens of the United States receive alternative and reliable sources of energy, and the rest of the world receive the fossil fuels that our nation will export. All of this could be achieved within ten years, as well. There is no partisan divide within this plan. If we as Americans can not rally behind a proposal to generate hundreds of billions of dollars, in addition to fixing our currently flawed energy system, I am unsure as to if we will ever be able to rally as one nation, under god.

CHAPTER FOUR
HEALTHCARE

"Don't go around saying the world owes you a living. The world owes you nothing. It was here first."
-Mark Twain

There is no question that the U.S. healthcare system needs reformation. As a matter of fact, I would call it one of the single largest issues that we face today. As much as I would like to believe that Obamacare had well intentions, despite the fact that, behind closed doors, drafters of the bill were caught calling Americans stupid for passing it, Obamacare has not been a success. A healthcare bill that mandated individuals to be insured still resulted in over 28 million Americans, or about 10% of the population, to be uninsured. Additionally, Obamacare punished these individuals with the dreaded individual mandate that taxed them at 2.5 % for not having health insurance. To the average household, that is an additional tax of about $1,4000 per year.

Additionally, Obamacare has not lowered insurance prices. The only aspect of health insurance that Obamacare has lowered has been competition, which is essential to free market success. Health insurance premiums have risen over 4% each year since Obamacare has been implemented, and in some areas there now are only one single health insurance provider. For reference, inflation has been about 1.8%.

The issue at hand here is not "greedy" insurance companies, as Bernie would like for you to believe, but rather a combination of a lack of true governance, as well as the pitiful health of general Americans. America currently has multiple epidemics, including the opioid epidemic, sugar/obesity epidemic, drug epidemic, and exercise epidemic.

Drug deaths have increased 60% overall in the last ten years, resulting in the death of over 48,000 Americans annually. This is equivalent to more than five deaths each hour. This is at the same time that billions of dollars ($50 billion annually, to be exact) are funneled into a failed war on drugs at the federal, state, and local levels. Obviously nobody would like to see Americans die in the streets due to drugs, as they currently are, but spending $50 billion annually inefficiently certainly does not solve the situation.

To begin to lower healthcare costs, we should first eliminate all spending on the war on drugs, and rather begin to collect billions of dollars annually upon the federal legalization of marijuana, and a tax of 25% on all sales. This tax would likely generate about $10 billion each year. This $10 billion could then be used to fight more serious drugs.

Next, the border must be secured, which is where 99.8% of many different illegal drugs come from. Finally, health insurance companies should have the right to ask individuals, under penalty of perjury, if they have every used, or currently use, illegal or legal drugs, and check the box of the drugs in which the have consumed or are consuming. Health insurance providers may then charge higher rates for these individuals, as they are exponentially more likely to use the services in which the health insurance provider provides.

On opiods, there are fairly simpler solutions. The opioid epidemic currently costs about $635 billion per year in lost potential productivity, as well as medical expenses. High-dose opioids should be banned, and legalized ones should not be prescribed so facetiously.

Furthermore, America has much more poor habits. 18.5% of Americans are excessive drinkers. Health insurance companies should have the right to charge more for these individuals, as it is almost certain that these individuals will have liver issues in the future. Additionally, 17.1% of Americans are smokers. These individuals, again, are almost certainly going to face catastrophic health issues in the future, and therefore should be charged more than those who do not smoke.

Additionally, a staggering 16.8% of Americans do not graduate high school. High school attendance should be compulsory nationwide, regardless of age. Even if you are 16 or 18, you should not be allowed to drop out. If you are caught off campus, you should be marked truant. College is called higher education for a reason, and that is the time in which classes should no longer have compulsory attendance. If individuals do not graduate high school, they are extremely limited in their options, and are exponentially more likely to partake in high risk behavior. Health insurance providers should begin to take highest level of education into account when providing individuals with quotes.

Next, and possibly most importantly, is the sugar or obesity epidemic within the U.S. According to the CDC, 37.9% of U.S. adults are obese, and 70.7% are overweight. More than 7 out of every 10 Americans are overweight. Obesity is now the leading cause of death in the U.S. The fact that health insurance companies can not examine weight/BMI when setting premiums is insane, as obesity is indeed a health crisis. If you are obese, you have a lower life expectancy, are at a higher risk of high blood pressure, high cholesterol, diabetes, heart disease, stroke, arthritis, sleep apnea, cancer, mental health issues, and an overall lower quality of life. Furthermore, obesity in the U.S. results in an estimated $150 billion in increased healthcare costs, annually, and since health insurance companies can not take obesity into account when setting premiums, this impacts all Americans.

It is essential that obesity rates in the U.S. drop, and Michelle Obama's school lunches did little to nothing to help the issue. To solve this epidemic, the federal government must encourage exercise. Individuals should exercise at least 60 minutes, or 1 hour, each day. This is critical, as it helps offset poor eating habits. Next, the government must have more ad campaigns promoting healthy lifestyles. These ad campaigns tend to be at least somewhat successful. Additionally, the appearance of nutrition labels should be edited. This is another thing that the Obama administration attempted to change for good, but ultimately did not. Michelle Obama's proposed nutrition label removed key aspects of the previous nutrition label, such as the actual recommended daily value of each ingredient. Next, GMO products should be labeled as such. Consumers have the right to know what they are consuming, afterall. Additionally, the FDA should edit the daily recommended values. They currently are not accurate, for two reasons. The first is that a 2,000 calorie diet is fairly high. Additionally, the FDA recommends consuming more fat than protein each day, and the overall recommendations are not accurate to maintain a healthy lifestyle. Additionally, many are unaware of the fact that what you see on a nutrition label may only be 80% accurate. The FDA allows companies to estimate the number of calories, fats, carbs, etc, within a 20% margin in either direction. This means that when your dinner says 800 calories, it could be 960, or it could be 640, or anywhere in between. This should be changed as well,

Finally, there are two ultimate steps that the federal government can take to aid in the decrease of overall obesity in the U.S. The first of these steps is extremely reformative. The federal government, particularly the USDA, should sell meals. They should operate a website, and it better not cost as much as the dysfunctional $2 billion Obamacare websites. On this website, individuals may purchase food items, each of which sold in packs, that contain the recommended nutritional values for breakfast, lunch, and dinner, based on age and weight goals. This website will be predicated upon a public-private partnership, with suppliers, as well as marketplaces, such as Amazon. The U.S. government will sell these food packs for the same price in which they purchase them at, and they will purchase them at a profit to companies. This ensures that no industries are impacted by federal involvement, as tends to be the case.

Secondly, and possibly most importantly, is the implementation of an extensive tax on all added sugars, nationwide. This will include but not be limited to candy, sugary drinks, energy drinks, etc. This tax will be set at 1 cent per gram. Organic sugars, such as fruits, will be exempt from the tax. The average American consumes about 152 pounds of sugar annually. This would equate to about a $690 tax on each American, assuming that the tax has no impact on their habits. If the tax does deter sugar consumption, that is positive as health would improve. If the sugar tax does not cut sugar consumption, at least the government will receive billions ($145 billion to be exact) to ensure a minimalized debt, in addition to increased spending on infrastructure, military, etc.

Additionally, there is exact legislation that will almost certainly lower premiums across the U.S. This begins with the abolition of defensive medicine. This is when doctors unnecessarily conduct tests or procedures, or prescribe medication, all in consternation of medical malpractice lawsuits. This alone is estimated to cost the U.S. economy approximately $700 billion each year. According to Gallup, one out of every four dollars spent on healthcare are directed towards this practice. This practice does absolutely nothing to improve the actual quality of care, but rather results in significantly increased prices. According to Vanderbilt University, in 2012, a staggering 96% of orthopedic surgeons stated that they engaged in defensive medicinal practices, which subsequently resulted in $2 billion in increased healthcare costs.

Furthermore, as is almost always the case, regulation should be lifted upon the healthcare industry. More specifically, unnecessary paperwork regulations. Currently, the process to receive prior authorization approval is over $80,000, per process. Annually, there are over 230,000 of these practices.

This equates to over $18 billion in additional costs, annually. The total cost, nationwide, of this wasted time is between $23 billion and $31 billion. Additionally, it is estimated that physicians spend two thirds of their time either filing or filling out paperwork. Doctors spend about 40 percent of their time on paperwork. The cost of this additional and unnecessary paperwork is an additional $83,000 per physician/doctor. If healthcare administrative overhead were to be cut in half, the result would be a subsequent saving of over $13 billion annually.

Moreover, an absolutely astonishing amount of money could be saved if reusable medical devices were mandated, as opposed to disposable devices. Reusable tools are just as efficient and effective, and save every party involved money. It is estimated that the cost of a disposable instruments per procedure is between 7 and 27 times more as the same procedure if it were to be conducted with reusable instruments. Due to the fact that there are over 48 million surgical procedures performed annually, the subsequent savings would be extraordinary. Additionally, it is estimated that the reusable instruments pay for themselves after a mer nine uses.

Finally, legislation that could aid in the lowering of medical costs overall can be found in superior surgical supply management. $48 billion each year could be saved if surgical waste were cut. Unused medical supplies ultimately account for 13 percent of total surgical supply costs. Additionally, costs could also be slashed by mandating an effective system in which surgeons are able to identify the tools in which they will use prior to performing the surgery, and leaving tools that are not expected to be used unopened. Seems fairly simple, right?

The FDA is the ultimate key to healthcare reformation within the U.S. It is undeniable and absolutely certain that the FDA currently is not favorable towards competition, AKA true free markets. Ideally, the FDA has an increased budget, in addition to an exponentially faster approval process, an increased number of employees, and an increased number of overall drug approvals. This should subsequently result in lower drug prices, overall. If we continue with the current system, which generates drug monopolies, we will never have lower prices. In Europe, there are alternatives to the Epipen. In the U.S, there is no such competition. The price of an Epipen in the U.S. is $600. In Europe, the price is $69. The exact same product, but a different market. Mylan, the owner of the Epipen, are not greedy, but rather genius, and comprehend that they can essentially force consumers to pay any price for their products.

Additionally, the U.S. should make drug importation much easier, and the FDA should conduct swift reviews upon drugs already approved by other agencies across the world. This would also increase competition, via the importation of innovation.

In summation, health insurance companies should have the right to examine a multitude of other factors than they currently are restricted to view. Additionally, more must be done to ensure that the health of Americans is drastically improved, and reformation is an absolute prerequisite to lower drug prices, as well as lower premiums. If done properly, pur currently flawed system can be fixed, but certainly not via current propositions.

CHAPTER FIVE
ABORTION

"Any society that will give up a little liberty to gain
a little security will deserve neither and lose both."
-Benjamin Franklin

Abortion, as a whole, is one of the most divided
political topics within the United States. According
to Gallup, 48% of Americans identify as pro-choice,
and another 48% identify as pro-life. This is an
exact split. The Supreme Court has, as of now,
stated that women do indeed possess a right to
abortion. However, in reference to morality,
abortion fails all tests.

It is immoral to end a pregnancy merely due to the
fact that you say so. It is comparable to refusing to
pay for a traffic infraction in which you are aware
that you committed. If not raped, or if there are no
other options for the mother (e.g. the woman will
via all means of delivering the baby), it is immoral
to have an abortion. However, there are plenty of
immoral laws. Legality is not basis for morality.

If one believes that the fetus does not possess a right
to live due to the fact that it is not a human, that is a
fair point. However, there are plenty of non-human
things that have rights and protections. Cats and
dogs are examples of such. A living thing does not
necessarily need to be a human if it is to possess
universal rights and values.

Additionally, the mother does not have a moral right to end a pregnancy due to any reasons or circumstances in which she desires. In 9 U.S. states, as well as Washington D.C, there is absolutely no limit to the time in which a woman may receive an abortion. It is legally possible to have a third trimester abortion in these states. Is that moral? Should that be legal, even?

Just recently, a baby born in the 21st week of pregnancy celebrated her first birthday. That baby was obviously capable of surviving, and not "just a cluster of cells". Even those who are "pro-choice" ultimately do agree that the fetus has value, the second that it comes out of the womb, at will. However, it is the role of society, not the parents nor guardians, to determine the value of a life. Legal or not, abortion as a whole is certainly immoral.

Finally, to what extent are abortions supported, even by those who are "pro-choice"? Hypothetically, if it could be determined whether or not a baby would be homosexual, and the mother predicted her decision as to whether or not to have an abortion on those sole results, would that be moral? Should that be allowed? If not, why not? It is no different from any other reason, such as poverty, illness, etc. The mother is generating children with desired traits, and the "undesired" children are rejected. That is why abortion should be illegal nationwide, after 12 weeks, barring exceptions of rape, or the identification of a newly developed basis for potential harm to the mother.

Furthermore, while on the topic of abortion, one may not skip over the largest abortion provider in the U.S: Planned Parenthood. If Mcdonald's is a monopoly in the fast food industry, then Planned Parenthood is the largest monopoly this country has ever seen, in the abortion industry. Believe it or not, this is the only field in which Planned Parenthood is even relative in relation to market share. Planned Parenthood may claim as many times as they wish that they are for "women's health", but they perform a mere 0.97% of America's total annual PAP tests, in addition to a disappointing 1.8% of America's total annual breast exams. However, this exact same "Women's health" agency is responsible for a staggering 30.6% of all abortions. For reference, Planned Parenthood commits 160 abortions for each child they refer to adoption.

Planned Parenthood is absolutely an abortion agency, calling them anything else is misleading. This includes the tremendous lie pertaining to the "3% of services". Planned Parenthood currently claims that abortion is only "3% of what they do". However, this is extremely misleading. This is due to the fact that, under this calculation, each clinical interaction is counted equally. This means that if you go into Planned Parenthood to get an abortion, and an ultrasound is performed prior to the abortion, Planned Parenthood would claim that "abortions are only 50% of what we do". Even if every single individual walked into Planned Parenthood to get an abortion, the overall number of abortions will not be 100%. This is entirely misleading, and Planned Parenthood knows this. Planned Parenthood deceives the uninformed in a scam to collect donations, and it has been working. If Planned Parenthood's logic were applied to the NFL, the NFL could say that, since they sold 1,000,000 hot dogs that year, but there were only 16 NFL games in the season, so therefore football is only 0.016% of "what they do".

Barring an overhaul of Roe v Wade, which would likely not be desirable, abortions can not legally be totally outlawed. However, regulation at the federal level is certainly necessary. There should be no time period during a pregnancy in which the baby is capable of surviving independently, or even via aid from physicians, and at the same time, it is possible for a woman to receive an abortion. That is cruel. Give women 12 weeks to develop a plan for their pregnancy, and it is as simple as that.

CHAPTER SIX
EDUCATION

"Education is the most powerful weapon which you can use to change the world."
-Nelson Mandela

There is absolutely no debating the fact that the current U.S. educational system is flawed. It is of general belief in America that being ranked 25th in both Reading and Science, and 40th in Mathematics, is absolutely not acceptable. However, despite these abismal rankings, the U.S. ranks 5th in per capita education spending. Instead of funneling billions of dollars into an obviously failed system, the current educational system must be reformed.

To begin, the teachers themselves should be treated differently. Currently, there is an immense lack of respect for teachers. Additionally, there is fairly low pay for most of these teachers, considering the fact that these teachers are responsible for training the next generation of American workers, and therefore creating the next economy. If these teachers fail at their job, we all fail.

It is for this reason that the performance of each teacher should be analyzed, and those deemed to be ineffective teachers should be fired. Currently, it is extremely difficult to do this, however, there must be a purge of these ineffective teachers, of which there are many. Assuming the average ineffective rate of approximately 1%, this purge will result in a subsequent firing of approximately 40,000 teachers, nationwide.

Next, it is essential that the U.S. decrease the teacher to student ratio, and therefore hire significantly more teachers, all of which highly trained. The current K-12 teacher to student ratio is approximately 23.1. Ideally, this number should be reduced to a mandated maximum of 20. No K-12 class should be allowed to have more, excluding P.E. This means that a total of about 600,000 new teachers must be brought into the workforce.

Finally, these teachers should be compensated significantly more than they currently are. It should be mandated that teachers make a minimum of two times the average salary of those within their designated household type. This means that if the teacher is single, and the average salary of those who are single is about $34,940, all single teachers must make at least $69,880, each year. This also means that, assuming annual wage growth is present, the salary of each teacher will increase annually, and at a more rapid rate than average.

Furthermore, the functionality of the current educational system must be reformed. If one examines the list of countries that rank highest in math, science, and reading, a universal trend will be recognized: the top countries are almost entirely

Asian. This is due to an array of factors, one of which being extremely stringent requirements to become a teacher. These requirements should not deter teachers from joining the workforce, but rather encourage the absolute best teachers to do so. These requirements should be implemented within the U.S.

Additionally, and potentially most importantly, is the difference between schedules in each nation that ranks above the U.S. In these other nations, there are no semesters, and no lengthy Summer breaks. Rather, school is broken into terms. Each term is three months long, with a one month break between each term. This should also be installed in the U.S. Trimesters, or terms, should be mandated, with the length of each being three months, or 60 school days. Currently, most states require 180 days of school, so this new schedule would not interfere with current mandates, but rather reform the schedule.

Furthermore, the length of each school day should be mandated. Each kindergarten school day should last at least 4 hours. During this time, retention is fairly low, but an array of essential topics should be introduced. Each elementary school day should last at least 7 hours, with one hour dedicated to lunch, and 30 minutes to a break. Each middle school day should last at least 8 hours. The schedule here must be comparable to high school in preparation for the transition to high school. Finally, each high school day should last at least 8 hours. Each class should be one hour long, with an additional hour dedicated towards passing periods/breaks, and another hour dedicated towards lunch. This new school day schedule, combined with trimester mandates, and a dramatic increase in the amount of teachers, as well as their overall salary, will almost certainly increase the U.S. global education ranking.

However, the above changes are only applicable to K-12 education. College, or higher education, must not be ignored either. Nevertheless, the U.S. actually ranks fairly high in overall higher education. The U.S. has, by far, the most universities in the global top 500. The U.S. has exponentially more than any two nations combined. However, the number of universities in the U.S. that reside within the top 500 is decreasing, in contrast to China, which is increasing at a rapid rate.

The only way that the U.S. could improve these numbers is via changes to policy amongst public universities/colleges, which tend not to rank within the top 500 to begin with. However, the focal point in reference to higher education is the price. Between 2002 and 2012, public university prices rose 39 percent, while private university prices rose 16 percent. Believe it or not, the private university price increases are much below the average rate of inflation within this time period (24.8 percent). The disproportional growth can be witnessed amongst the public sector, not the private. Nonetheless, it is possible to lower overall prices for both public and private universities.

Currently, there are over $1.48 trillion in outstanding student loans, with $1.33 trillion of these loans coming from the federal government. Due to the fact that this debt is already accounted for, the national debt would not be impacted by a total and absolute forgiveness of all federal student loans. Rather, the economy would likely increase as debt holders would be burdened by the debt, and earn less of a salary.

This is exactly what should occur. However, upon doing so, the federal student loan program should be indefinitely abolished, and failure to pay private student loans should result in tremendously harsh punishment. An abolition of the federal student loan program will result in the loss of a guarantee that college, at current prices, will be able to be funded. This should result in a subsequent drop in overall prices at private universities, since, from their perspective, previous federal loan policies essentially guaranteed that, no matter the price in which they charged, the money would be available to them. Now, however, certain individuals may not qualify, as a private bank is much less inclined to hand out thousands of dollars to individuals who likely will not pay their debts.

Furthermore, the federal government should increase the number of grants they provide into

STEM majors. It is critical that the U.S. lead in the STEM sector if they are to remain dominant throughout the next generation. The federal government should not support absolutely silly majors, such as gender studies, puppetry, etc. These majors are not meaningful at all, and the "knowledge/skills" obtained could be obtained via like minded individuals gathering upon forming a Facebook group. It is an absolute waste of money and is a complete embarrassment of what current college campuses have become.

Current federal pell grant spending is approximately $22.4 billion annually. This number should be decreased to $20 billion. However, a new grant should be given to any individual who chooses a STEM major. This grant should be of $7,500 each year. This will result in approximately $18 billion in new funding. However, funding for this grant will come directly from the elimination of the federal student loan program, which currently costs an estimated $18 billion annually.

Assuming each individual step above is taken with regard to education, higher education prices will surely decrease, the overall quality of education, and therefore the U.S. global educational ranking, will increase, and the general life of each and every American will increase in caliber.

CHAPTER SEVEN
ECONOMICS

"One thing is clear: the Founding Fathers never intended a nation where citizens would pay nearly half of everything they earn to the government. "
-Ron Paul

The economy is the single most important current issue within our country, shortly ahead of intensive divisiveness and security. No nation can become nor remain a superpower without a powerful economy, and no economy can become truly powerful that is not capitalistic. Capitalism is the focal point to all truly fair and truly great economies.

However, in the U.S, capitalism is becoming less and less popular each day, especially amongst younger citizens. According to a recent Harvard University poll, 51 percent of Americans aged 18 years old to 29 years old opposed capitalism, while a mere 41 percent expressed support for capitalism. While certain general critiques of capitalism may be fair, what is even more confounding is the general love and admiration for the absolute worst economic system the world has ever witnessed: socialism/communism. 44 percent of millenials would prefer to live in a socialist country, while 42 percent would prefer to live in a capitalistic society.

Before addressing the flaws of all economic systems, besides capitalism, the excellence of capitalism must first be addressed.

To begin, capitalism is absolutely morally superior to every other economic system, for an array of reasons. The first of these is the overall promotion of freedom. Capitalism allows all individuals to experience freedom of choice. Capitalism allows individuals to determine whether or not they wish to purchase an item, in addition to the amount of items in which they would like to purchase, where individuals wish to live, where individuals wish to work, where they wish to purchase from, and so on. Under socialism, or statism, the government mandates, and therefore infringes upon, these freedoms. A loss of choice is an absolute reduction in overall freedom, and if all choice is revoked, that, by definition, is slavery. Statism/socialism is one step closer to slavery.

Next, capitalism promotes cooperation, in addition to compromisation. If one wanted to renovate their home, they would contact a contractor, and would then agree upon a price for the overall job. If one agrees to this price, it is due to the fact that they value the services in which they are receiving more than they do the money in their pockets, otherwise, they would not accept the offer. On the other hand, the contractor considers which he or she values more, the amount of money he or she will recieve, or the overall requirements to perform the task, including, but not limited to, time and labor. Under statism/socialism, there is no such cooperation. Individuals are punished for challenging the state, and the individuals who are not punished must therefore comply with the commands of the state. An example can be seen in both price and wage control, such as the minimum wage.

Entry level jobs, which tend to subsequently be minimum wage jobs, are the absolute first step on the employment ladder. These jobs tend to therefore teach employees essential skills that sadly are not taught in school, such as teamwork and money management. If an entry level individual were to seek work, they would likely, rightfully so, not receive hefty compensation. Perhaps, one may not even want to hire them, at least not at the current minimum wage, due to the fact that one values their money more than the services of that individual. However, under a truly free system, the state would not impose a minimum wage, and a salary could be negotiated, one in which both parties agree to. That is true freedom. That is true liberty. That is true capitalism.

Furthermore, capitalism is exponentially more optimistic than all other economic systems. Under capitalism, there is no limit to which you can not succeed, and there is always room to improve. A capitalist are always looking for potential gains, potential expansion, and overall opportunities. This general promotion of creation, and therefore success, is exponentially more moral than the suppression of the future, known as statism/socialism.

Additionally, capitalism promotes individualism. Capitalism, as a whole, puts trust in each individual to make their own decisions. Statism/socialism does not allow individuals to make individual decisions, and therefore believes that an elite force (the state) must make decisions for such individuals. Structurally, capitalism trusts the common man, despite any flaws. Socialism/statist belittles individuals. Capitalism is certainly morally superior.

Next, capitalism is morally superior by reason of the fact that capitalism supports equality. Critics may questions "income inequality", whose existence is factual, but this inequality is not systematic. The equality that is systematically integrated within capitalism is equal opportunity. Not everyone is equal in skillset. If one were to attempt to play a basketball game against Michael Jordan, they would lose ten times out of ten. One could call the result "unfair", or they could do what Michael Jordan did: train, work hard, and strive for excellence until excellence is achieved, and even then, one must not stop. Capitalism promotes growth, and an opportunity for any individual to become successful. Statism/socialism, however, would examine Michael Jordan, and would come to the concussion that his skills are "unfair".

Statists/socialists would then claim that Michael Jordan must be handicapped somehow, in order to make the game "fair". They may claim that Michael Jordan must give some of the points that he scores to the other team. This, however, does not help the other team. Rather, the other team has less of a reason to try, after all, why would they? No matter what, they will get the points that Jordan earns.

Income inequality is not a legitimate inequality. Afterall, a poor man today is not necessarily a poor man tomorrow. This, however, is only true under capitalism. To quote the great Winston Churchill: "The inherent vice of capitalism is the unequal sharing of blessings; the inherent virtue of socialism is the equal sharing of miseries." Due to the fact that capitalism focus on opportunity, rather than result, capitalism is considerably more moral.

Furthermore, capitalism supports emulation. Socialists/statists resent the rich, whereas capitalists wish to emulate them. Resentment and envy can be tremendously dangerous. Emulation is exponentially more moral than envy. Capitalism is much more moral than socialism/statism.

Additionally, those who are successful under capitalism provide other individuals value. In a genuinely capitalistic society, the only potential way in which a business may prosper is if individuals voluntarily trade with such a business for the services in which the business offers.

Furthermore, the only way for such business to expand is if they improve the products or services in which they offer. If a business ultimately put their interests above the interests of consumers, the business will certainly fail. Consequently, capitalism is a competition of giving. Naturally, some self interest is involved in capitalism, but capitalism funnels the self interest into selflessness. The only way in which entrepreneurs/companies may succeed is if they help others. Capitalistic wealth comes from a correlation between the amount of value in which you generate for others. Statist/socialist wealth is derived from exploited positions and connections to higher officials. Wealth that is value driven is much more moral than wealth that is driven by elite corruption.

Finally, capitalism is morally superior to statism/socialism due to the fact that capitalism promotes human nature. If one were told that they would receive the same amount of compensation, no matter their level of contribution, they would likely not work very hard. This is due to an overall lack of incentive. Incentive is rooted within capitalism, and each incentive serves the public as a whole. Statists/socialists suppress incentives. Capitalism respects and encourages human nature, and is therefore morally superior.

There are an array of reasons as to why socialism/statism is absolutely not a desirable economic system. The first of these is the fact that statism/socialism is extremely condescending. Socialism/statism removes the individual liberty involved in decision making. Socialism/statism inherently believes that individuals lack the intellectual capacity to decide for themselves the extent to which they do or do not need items/services.

Next, socialism is an undesirable economic system due to the fact that the system as a whole is inefficient. By removing incentives, in addition to the partial or total elimination of private ownership, basic economic success becomes impossible. The federal government is not an economy, and no government can become such. It is impossible. The nations of the former USSR, Cuba, Vietnam, Venezuela, and North Korea have attempted such an economic system, and not a single system was stable and successful.

Socialism/statism kills economic growth, which is the focal point of job creation, tax revenue, an a general increased standard of living for all individuals. Socialism/statism punishes growth, and rewards failure/laziness. Nature does not function this way, for obvious reasons. If nature were to operate this way, a collapse would be inevitable as dependency would be certain. This is the reason why signs are displayed that state not to feed the birds, as doing so creates a dependent population.

Next, socialism/statism is an objectionable economic system by virtue of the fact that it coerces governments to become progressively tyrannical. Socialism/statism requires tremendous levels of bureaucracy, and these bureaucracies always grow exponentially larger. As the bureaucracies grow, the more centralized the government becomes, and therefore the more ominous the government becomes.

Socialism/statism may appear as though they are successful shortly after their implementation. However, this is merely due to the fact that not all of the income has been diluted from successful individuals, yet. The more money that is taken from successful people nad given to poorer individuals in society, naturally, the total number of successful individuals decreases. This generates a cycle in which more people become in need of statist/socialist support, and therefore more money must be taken. Believe it or not, socialism actually increases the concentration of wealth, as most of the upper class is diluted to essentially nothing, but the extremely rich become exponentially richer, relative to the rest of society. The economy will then soon begin to slow down, as the economy will no longer be capable of generating an adequate amount of revenue to sustain itself. This is exactly what happened to the USSR, exactly what happened to Greece, exactly what happened to Venezuela, and exactly what will happen to the next nation foolish enough to ignore these facts.

While it is indeed factual that capitalism is the greatest economic system known to man, there are some flaws pertaining to the U.S. version of capitalism. Contrary to common belief, the U.S. is not fully capitalistic. This is for an array of reasons, one of which being the presence of a central bank. The central bank of the U.S. is known as the Federal Reserve.

The Federal Reserve artificially stalls growth of the U.S. economy. This is exactly what Karl Marx wished for when hec called for "Centralization of credit in the hands of the state, by means of a national bank with State capital and an exclusive monopoly." The Federal Reserve is an absolute monopoly of private banks, and if one were interested in learning more about the Federal Reserve's history, they should read "The Truth About The Fed", by Parker Bono.

Regardless, there is no debating the fact that the Federal Reserve has communist roots, and is absolutely not capitalistic. Furthermore, there should be little debate over the proper fate of the Federal Reserve: the Federal Reserve should cease to exist. The U.S. Treasury should print and distribute dollars and coins, rather than merely printing currency for the Federal Reserve to manipulate to generate artificial growth.

The next flaw of current U.S, capitalism can be seen in protectionist policies, particularly, tariffs. Tariffs are not truly capitalistic. True capitalism refers to free trade, with absolutely zero protectionist policies. If every major nation were to sign a declaration promising the elimination of all tariffs, truly free trade would be possible.

Tariffs are essentially a tax on consumers, collected by their own government. While this tax may discourage the purchase of particular products, the government should never attempt to sway consumers as to which products they should or should not purchase, especially via artificially increased prices. This same rule should apply to other nations, as well.

Additionally, any trade deficit is not a "loss" for the U.S. Nobody is losing money. All trade is mutually beneficial, if the trade is completed freely. The $375 billion trade deficit with China can be explained simply: the U.S. imported approximately $505 billion in goods from China that ultimately were beneficial to the U.S. as a whole, and China imported approximately $130 billion of tremendous American goods that were ultimately beneficial to China. The difference of approximately $375 billion was subsidized via the sale of stocks, bonds, assets, or even loans to the Chinese. Delivering the Chinese assets in exchange for imports is not a loss anymore than a loan from a car dealership to purchase a vehicle. In each situation, buyers predict that they will benefit from the trade, regardless of the source of the purchasing funds.

The nation/individual who enacted the first tariff is an absolute moron, as they obviously lacked the intellectual capacity to comprehend the fact that every action has an equal opposite reaction. However, it is understandable why any nation, particularly the U.S, would attempt to enact tariffs as a method of reducing trade deficits. After All, there is not much in which the U.S. could possibly lose. An ultimate trade war to end all trade wars/tariffs is absolutely comprehensible, and even logical. However, upon completion of this ultimate trade war, via the signage of a declaration to end all tariffs, that declaration shall never be infringed, or true free trade will be jeopardized once again.

In an ideal society, the economic system is capitalistic. The taxes, and government intervention as a whole, are low. There is no central bank comprised of private banks, and there are no tariffs. If a nation were entirely free trade, lacked the existence of a central bank, had low government intervention, and low tax rates, the nation would be the greatest economy the world has ever seen. Additionally, the economic growth of such a nation would be sustainable, unlike the artificial growth witnessed in the U.S, and across the globe. The 1,000,000 percent inflation rate in Venezuela is not sustainable, and neither is any socialist/statist economy.

CHAPTER EIGHT
ALLIANCES

"Peace, commerce, and honest friendship with all
nations-entangling alliances with none."
-Thomas Jefferson

The above quote may have originated from the 18th
century, but the quote is just as relevant today. The
U.S, and no other nation with any moderate level of
intelligence, should align themselves in
non-expiring, and therefore entangling, alliances.

The first of these many alliances that impact the
U.S. is NATO. The first of innumerable problems
with NATO is ANTO's recent expansion. NATO
was originally created by the U.S, Canada, and
many other European nations in 1949, in order to
defend against the Soviet Union in. Since the
collapse of the Soviet Union was fairly apparent, as
were the Soviet Union's keen hatred for Europe, a
key ally to the U.S, a temporary alliance at this time
would be absolutely justified.

However, the Soviet Union no longer exists, and
neither should European fears of Russian invasion.
Expanding NATO does absolutely nothing other
than proliferate Russian aggressiveness. Despite the
fact that Russia's actions are absolutely unjustified,
it is an utter fact that Russia immensely values the
nations in which NATO recently added. This
includes Georgia, Montenegro, and, potentially,

Ukraine. This is comparable to the Soviet Union inviting Canada and Mexico to join the Warsaw Pact.

Additionally, the U.S. is the absolute focal point of the alliance, yet the U.S. tends to act the most pusillanimous at meetings. The combined GDP of NATO member nations is about $36.25 trillion. The U.S. represents $16.35 trillion, or about 45%, of this overall figure. However, even when the data is adjusted for proportionality, the U.S. is still exploited. Every NATO member is expected to spend at least 2% of their respected GDP on defense. Depressingly, only five nations of the twenty nine, the U.S, greece, Poland, Estonia, and the United Kingdom, hit the expected quota. Seven nations, however, spend less than 1% of GDP on defense. These numbers are absolutely despicable and unacceptable. The U.S, can not, and should not, spend $650 billion of the $900 billion in defense spending.

There is absolutely nothing wrong with spending an excess amount of money on defense, the U.S. should continue to do so. However, there is an issue with supposedly allied nations exploiting the U.S, and not meeting the obligations in which they agreed and promised to fulfil. To quote the great Lord Salisbury, "Isolation is much less dangerous than the danger of being dragged into wars which do not concern us." The above quote was from

1896, but, as is such with many quotes, is just as relevant today.

If the U.S. is to remain in NATO, two things must occur. Firstly, the 2% of GDP "target" needs to become mandatory. All NATO members must contribute 2% of GDP, or they will no longer be NATO members. Finally, an amendment must be made that states that the treaty of NATO as a whole is to be dissolved every ten years, with the possibility of renewal. The U.S. can no longer be involved in endless and therefore entangling alliances. If the U.S. is to remain in NATO, they definitely should not make concessions when the other member nations are dependents of the U.S.

The next alliance that shall be targeted is the United Nations. According to Gallup, a mere 34% of Americans believe that the United Nations has done an overall good job in solving the issues in which they face, whereas 60% of Americans claimed that the United Nations did a poor job. President Trump has higher approval numbers than the approval of the performance of the United Nations.

Anyways, there are not very many overall issues with the United Nations as a whole. However, the alliance as a whole should be made temporary, just as NATO should be. The United Nations should be dissolved each ten years, with the possibility of readmission for all nations who wish to return for another ten year period.

Next, as is such with trade wars, it is essential that the U.S. fight a debt war of epic proportions. It shall be the debt war to end all debt wars. The U.S. national debt may seem impossible to pay off. Some argue that the only way to pay off such an astounding debt that totals over $20 trillion is to shrink federal spending. While shrinking federal spending is certainly desirable, there is one other method that is exponentially simpler. If the U.S. were to demand that every nation that owed the U.S. money paid such debt within one year, the U.S. would collect approximately $15.3 trillion.

Assuming that all other nations retaliated with a similar response, and demanded that the U.S. pay all debt that it owes, the U.S. would need to pay $18.4 trillion. While this is indeed a net loss, it would immediately result in a national debt reduction of over 70%. This would bring the new national debt total to approximately $6 trillion, including all sources. The U.S. should then pass legislation prohibiting more spending than revenues, each year. This will essentially resolve the debt issue.

Next, and possibly most importantly, is the issue of our so called allies. It is a fact that America currently has no true ally. Historically, France absolutely meets the definition of an ally, and throughout world wars, true allies have been present, but currently, the U.S. lacks a real ally.

The U.S. may have certain nations in which they have dominated historically, such as Japan, that may now indeed be a friend, but, by definition, they are no ally. An ally provides mutual military support to the United States, and contributes to the U.S. to make them safer. No nation does such, but the U.S. absolutely does. The U.S. has bought every single friend in which it currently possess, whether via force or via money, or a combination of both.

Even NATO, our closest example to an ally, is not a true ally. How the hell does Montenegro, a corrupt nation with a population of less than 650,000, contribute to the security of the U.S? Montenegro's GDP is less than $4.2 billion. The U.S. spends that in less than three days on defense alone. The U.S. is fully capable of defending themselves, and they do not need to be entangled to Montenegro, or any NATO ally for that matter.

Israel exists because of the U.S, and they should continue to exist. However, there is absolutely no question that Israel would not stand today if it weren't for the U.S. However, the U.S. absolutely would remain standing if it weren't for Israel. Israel is a key friend, and key to the region they reside upon, but they are not an ally. No nation is.

The main reason that the U.S. "needs" allies, and attempts to buy allies, is not due to the defense of the U.S, but rather the defense of those very allies. It is essentially a self licking ice cream cone. The

U.S. has no ally, and does not really need any allies. Our many tremendous friends are indeed greatly appreciated, and indeed necessary, but they are extremely different from allies.

However, if the U.S. is to have any allies, they must provide mutual defense to the U.S, and therefore must be comparable in size, particularly millitairly, and preferably economically. Three main nations, potentially four, meet such requirements. The United States. China, Russia, and India. A treaty or agreement between these four nations would be truly astounding. This coalition would be absolutely unstoppable in all aspirations.

Combining the military prowess of each nation would result in 5.8 million frontline soldiers, which exceeds the entire population of ten NATO member nations, over 40,000 tanks, over 22,000 aircrafts, and over 200 submarines. Additionally, the combined economies of these nations represents over $35.5 trillion, or over 44% of global GDP, and each of these nations are growing at an above average rate, excluding Russia. However, both Russia and the U.S. would grow at an exceedingly quicker rate if they were to remove sanctions on one another, which would also make Russia much more inclined to cooperate with U.S. requests.

A ten year alliance between the nations of the United States, China, Russia, and India is essential to ensure global dominance, and innovation. Such an alliance would also aid in domestic growth and prosperity, as well. Finally, this alliance would also pioneer a path to both domestic and global peace. These new nations would be the first true allies of the U.S. in many decades.

Ideally, the U.S. ensures that all treaties in which they sign have a term of dissolution, with the potential of renewal. No treaty/agreement/alliance should be indefinite. Additionally, the U.S. should use it's leverage within NATO to mandate the 2% funding "target". Finally, the U.S. must ally, temporarily, of course, with China, India, and Russia. If the above were implemented, the U.S. as a whole, in addition to the world, would be an exponentially safer and more prosperous place.

CHAPTER NINE
CIVIL LIBERTIES

"Those who would give up essential Liberty, to purchase a little temporary Safety, deserve neither liberty nor safety."
-Benjamin Franklin

The first amendment to the U.S. Constitution pertains to civil liberties. The Constitution is fairly clear as to the definition and extent of such liberties, but since some individuals today seem not to be capable of comprehending, or respecting, the Constitution, clarification is needed.

To begin, the freedom of speech is the first and main civil liberty of discussion in current politics. Many individuals claim that there is such a thing as "hate speech". Some even go as far to claim that such speech is not, or should not be protected speech. These individuals could not be farther from the truth. The Supreme Court unanimously affirmed that "hate speech" is protected speech. To quote justice Samuel Alito, "[The idea that the government may restrict] speech expressing ideas that offend … strikes at the heart of the First Amendment. Speech that demeans on the basis of race, ethnicity, gender, religion, age, disability, or any other similar ground is hateful; but the proudest boast of our free speech jurisprudence is that we protect the freedom to express "the thought that we hate.""

While most individuals would likely agree upon how to define "hate speech", the definition is as useful as a definition from Urban Dictionary, as there is no legal definition, and "hate speech" laws have been ruled unconstitutional. The U.S, with all of its flaws, is the greatest nation on the face of the Earth. The main reason for such a fact is the first amendment. Other nations may indeed have freedom of speech, but not to the same extent as the U.S, and the right is certainly not a focal point of their Constitution. This difference is one of the multiple of American exceptionalism. So long as one's speech does not incite violence, it is, and should be, legal.

Next, and possibly the most candid, is the freedom of religion. All people within the U.S. have the right to worship whatever religion they wish, or even not worship at all. While each individual has the right to religion, dialogue between those of different religions should absolutely remain. Finally, it should be noted that religion is an extremely divisive topic, which is the absolute last thing that the U.S. needs at the moment. Nobody should give a damn about the religious belief or affiliation of others, it is their belief, and they have the absolute right to believe in what they wish. Attacking/demeaning/stereotyping any religion, whether christian or muslim or jewish, or whatever, may be legal, and in some cases make a good joke, but it certainly is not desirable for a nation attempting to heal its wounds of division. Furthermore, Americans have the right to assembly. This one is also fairly simple, although some individuals today protest at improper locations and at improper times. One has a right to protest peacefully, and without disrupting the public. However, it is an absolute disruption to protest on a road, and one should expect to be hit when committing such an action. If an individual wishes to remain in their car, and not protest, one can not force them to exit their vehicle. This is essentially what occured in Charlottesville, Virginia. A car was on the road, and ignorant and moronic protestors were as well. As a result of their ignorant, and later violent, actions, some individuals whom were on the road were hit. Both prior to and upon impact, protestors were touching, hitting, kicking, and even swinging at, the Dodge Charger. The driver then accelerated into reverse upon his vehicle being struck multiple times, once again. Was this outcome desirable? Absolutely not. Was this outcome perhaps unnecessary? Yes. Was this outcome legal? I would argue so, and I predict that, barring immense juror bias, the "attacker" will be found not guilty. This situation could have been entirely avoided if individuals followed the law, and protested on the sidewalk, or in a designated area, rather than the street.

Additionally, individuals have the right to petition. As is the case with everything, there is a process to everything. This includes getting a law passed. There is little question or even debate about the right to petition. Ideally, this remains the case in the coming years.

Finally, and certainly essential to our nation, is the freedom of press. While freedom of the press is unquestionable, there are indeed limitations. The first of such is the right to the overall access of information. The media has no right to every piece of information within government control, according to the Supreme court. The next limitation pertains to the publication of obscenity, and national security risks or threats. While these terms are immensely vague, and therefore fairly difficult to prosecute, these limitations still exist. Finally, and absolutely most importantly, is the issue of libel. There have been multiple monumental libel cases. In *Milkovich v. Lorain Journal Co,* for example, it was revealed that even opinion pieces can be subject to libel. A wrestling coach from Ohio was involved within a fight, and there was later a criminal investigation. A reporter wrote about the coach, and described him as a "liar". The Supreme Court ruled that the coach could sue. This is now why reporters use vague phrases, as they are less likely to be indicted for libel cases. Additionally, in *Gertz v. Robert Welch, Inc*, it was ruled that even public figures may sue publications for libel. A lawyer, whom was also a public figure, was called a "leninist" by a publication. In response to the subsequent lawsuit, the publication argued that,

since the lawyer was a public figure, the malice
standard was not applicable. The Supreme Court
disagreed with the publication, and allowed the
lawyer to sue. Overall, libel laws should absolutely
be tightened. Far too many times are stories
published that are just total and complete garbage.
They are entirely fake, biased, and merely written to
attempt to damage the reputation of the individual.
Freedom of the press, in addition to freedom of
speech, are essential to the U.S. However, as is the
integrity of journalists, and the right of individuals
to not be intimidated and ruined by the media.

Overall, the first amendment to the Constitution is
possibly the most essential to freedom and liberty.
The first amendment must remain intact, as it has
historically. The U.S. can not allow "hate speech"
to undermine fundamental values.

CHAPTER TEN
IMMIGRATION

"Immigration laws are the only laws that are discussed in terms of how to help people who break them."
-Thomas Sowell

Illegal immigration as a whole is one of the largest issues that the U.S. faces. Nothing illegal should be encouraged. Yet, many individuals do indeed encourage the crime of immigrating to the U.S. illegally. Immigration as a whole is indeed amazing and should be welcomed, but only when done legally. As stated previously, there is a process to everything.

Some individuals who certainly are not of so much as mildly average IQ claim that "humans can not be illegal". While this is essentially true, this is not what is being referred to. It is a fact that an individual's legal status within a nation can be described as undocumented, or illegal, if they did not migrate here legally. It is extremely simple and easy to comprehend.

A nation without borders, by definition, is no longer a nation. It is essential that our border is secured and that the rule of law is enforced. If one truly believes in the Constitution, they believe that even the laws in which they disagree with must be enforced. For example, slavery. Slavery was horrendous and absolutely unacceptable, and I would be one of the first individuals to advocate for abolition of slavery. However, until the law were changed, I would respect such a law. The same goes for Obamacare. I do not support Obamacare as a whole, and would love to see the legislation as a whole repealed, however, until that is done, the law must be respected and enforced.

Firstly, the overall costs of illegal immigration must be addressed. These costs are astronomical. According to the Congressional Budget Office, "the tax revenues that unauthorized immigrants generate for state and local governments do not offset the total cost of services provided to them". However, "in aggregate and over the long term, tax revenues of all types generated by immigrants—both legal and unauthorized—exceed the cost of the services they use." Unauthorized immigrants demand goods and services while an estimated 50 to 75 percent pay taxes. Due to cheaper labor, they contribute to lower prices in the industries where they work, such as agriculture, restaurants, and construction." Notice how unauthorized/illegal immigrants have a net positive cost on the system, whereas legal immigrants have a net negative impact, and contribute extensively to the U.S.

This is not to say in any way whatsoever that illegal immigrants do not work. Many of them are potentially the hardest workers on the planet. However, it is factual that these illegal immigrants are willing to work so hard that they will take pay cuts. Therefore, legal employees must also take pay cuts to compete for the same position.

Overall, it is estimated that illegal immigrants cost the federal government approximately $45.8 billion each year, and cost state and local governments an additional $89 billion. This is a total cost of about $134.8 billion. However, there are some illegal immigrants who do indeed pay taxes. It is estimated that illegal immigrants pay approximately $14.5 billion annually in federal taxes, and an additional $3.5 billion in state and local taxes. This brings the net cost of illegal immigrants to about $120 billion, each year. Now a $10 billion, or even $20 billion wall does not seem so bad.

If the U.S. is to properly enforce its immigration laws, renovation is an absolute necessity at the southern border. Whether a wall, cameras, drones, more ICE agents, whatever it is, further defense is necessary. If President Trump did not campaign on building a wall, the Democrats would support funding for a wall. Afterall, they have supported funding for such a barrier for years since Trump. Particularly, when former President Obama deported more illegal immigrants than any other President in the history of the United States.

Next, it is essential that the topic of "family separation" is brought up. Ideally, are families separated? Absolutely not. However, it is either separate the children, or keep the parents) and children) together in jail. Or, the U.S. can avoid the entire scandal as a whole if the individuals were immediately deported. There are currently over 2.7 million children in the U.S. with an incarcerated parent. This is immensely sad, but the U.S. can not change the laws because they impact families negatively. If the U.S. were to, no law would remain. When a parent commits a crime, they are held responsible. When the child is taken, they are separated from their parent, because they did not commit the crime, at least not knowingly. Once again, this is an example of an extremely simple issue blown out of proportion and taken out of context by individuals of subpar IQ.

Furthermore, and most importantly, is the issue of legal immigration. Currently, the U.S. takes in about 1 million legal immigrants each year. This number is absolutely acceptable, and, if amended somewhat, could actually be increased. However, a cap/limit of annual immigration is necessary, as are a few reformations to the current immigration system, as a whole.

First, a cap/limit of 0.35% of the population from the last census should be implemented. Currently, this would equate to slightly over 1.1 million legal immigrants, or a 10% increase in annual legal immigration. This slight increase will ultimately be beneficial.

Next, an overall merit based system of admission should be implemented. This means that every individual who applies will be given a score, based on an array of details, such as criminal history, current language spoken, college degree, amount of children/dependents, and net worth. The higher the score, the higher an individual rises on the merit rankings. At the end of the year, the top number of individuals that reach the quote (0.35% of population) are admitted, and the rest are turned down, for this immigration cycle. This will ensure that the individuals who have the most to offer are taken into the U.S. as quickly as possible., and will therefore ensure that the U.S. as a whole becomes even more successful due to the new immigration system.

Finally, the U.S. should mandate a response time of one year to all legal applicants. This means that within one year, each individual who applied for citizenship/residence will receive a response of either acceptance or denial. This will eliminate the horrible current waiting period, in which some individuals spend half of their lives waiting due to a failed system. This system would also deter illegal immigrants from crossing illegally, as they would obviously prefer to be legal, and would have an exponentially swifter response time than the current system.

As a whole, the immigration laws within the U.S. should be followed. It is critical that the U.S. have strong and efficient borders if they are to remain a strong and efficient nation. Additionally, the border must be secured via the implementation of innovative technology. Next, the U.S. should implement a merit bascd system in which legal immigrants are accepted into the U.S. This system should have an admission cap of 0.35% of the population from the previous census. Finally, each legal applicant should be mandated to receive a response of either acceptance or denial within one year of applying. If each of the above were to be implemented, the U.S. as a whole would become considerably more prosperous, and illegal immigration would certainly be cut, overall.

SOURCES

Chapter One

*The Washington Times, U.S. Tax Code Longer
Than Bible-Without Good News, January 9, 2013*

*The Tax Foundation, The Compliance Costs Of IRS
Regulations, June 15, 2016*

*CNBC, The Average American Made $44.6K Last
Year, October 20, 2015*

*The Heritage Foundation, The Historical Lessons
Of Lower Tax Rates, August 13, 2003*

*Time, John F. Kennedy And Ronald Reagan Proved
Tax Cuts Work, September 29, 2016*

*The Tax Foundation, Corporate Income Tax Rates
Around The World, September 7, 2017*

*The Motley Fool, The Average American Has This
401(k) Balance. How Do You Compare?, October
10, 2016*

*The National Bureau Of Economic Research,
Simulating The Elimination Of The U.S. Corporate
Income Tax*

*The Atlantic, Why We Should Eliminate The
Corporate Income Tax, October 28, 2010
Forbes, 6 Reasons Trump Should Abolish
Corporate Income Tax, December 19, 2016*

*The Washington Times, End Corporate Income Tax,
November 20, 2004*

*The Tax Foundation, New Study Ponders
Elimination Of The Corporate Income Tax, April
11, 2014*

*Bamboo Core, The Average American Consumes
150-170 Pounds Of Sugar Each Year*

*The New York Times, Numbers Tell Of Failure In
Drug War, July 3, 2012*

*Fortune, Colorado Topped $1 Billion In Legal
Marijuana Sales In 2016, December 13, 2016*

*Statista, U.S. Online Gambling Industry - Statistics
And Facts*

Wikipedia, Fuel Taxes In The United States

AAA, Gas Prices

The Wall Street Journal, Abolish The Gas Tax, January 14, 2015

IRS, Estate Tax, 2017

The Tax Foundation, The Economics Effects Of The Estate Tax, October 17, 2011

The Heritage Foundation, The Case For Repealing The Estate Tax, August 21, 1996

Joshua Kennon, 1,821,745 Households In The United States Have Investment Portfolios Worth $3,00,000 Or More, July 18, 2015

CBS, Government Spending Per Minute: $6.85 Million, January 7, 2011

Gallup, Smoking

Tax Policy Center, Tobacco Tax Revenue, October 18, 2017

The Tax Foundation, The Effect Of The Federal Cigarette Tax Increase On State Revenue, April 1, 2009
NPR, Hidden Brain: How Cigarette Taxes Affect Food Buying, July 25, 2017

Chapter Two

Live Science, The Second Amendment & The Right To Bear Arms, June 28, 2017

Constitution Society, The Meaning Of The Phrase "Well Regulated" In The 2nd Amendment

Cornell Law School, 10 U.S. Code § 246

The Daily Caller, These Guns Dispel The Notion The Founding Fathers Could Never Have Imagined Modern Assault Rifles, June 29, 2016

Time, A Criminologist's Case Against Gun Control, December 1, 2015

NPR, Rate Of U.S. Gun Violence Has Fallen Since 1993, Study Finds, May 7, 2013

Politifact, Greg Abbott Says That According To FBI, More People Are Killed Each Year With Clubs, Hammers Than With Rifles, January 30, 2013

Forbes, These Are The U.S. Billionaires Who Back Gun Control, June 15, 2016

Chapter Three

EIA, The United States Uses A Mix Of Energy Sources

Stanford, Building A Nuclear Plant, March 19, 2017

EIA, What Is U.S. Electricity Generation By Source?

Intergovernmental Panel on Climate Change, Special Report on Renewable Energy and Climate Change Mitigation, 2011

City Lab, The Environmentalist Case Against 100% Renewable Energy Plans, July 20, 2015

Canadian Nuclear Association, Nuclear Power Saves Lives: Six Quick Facts

Newsweek, Three Mile Island Accident Deaths, Location: Facts On Nuclear Meltdown Anniversary, March 28, 2018

The Washington Post, Romney Would Open Federal Lands To Drilling. How Much Oil And Gas Is There?, August 25, 2012

Chapter Four

Bloomberg, Obamacare Website Costs Exceed $2 Billion, Study Finds, September 24, 2014

Forbes, ACA Architect: "The Stupidity Of The American Voter" Led Us To Hide Obamacare's True Costs From Public, November 10, 2014

Commonwealth Fund, U.S. Physician Practices Spend Nearly Four Times as Much Money Interacting with Health Plans and Payers Than Do Their Canadian Counterparts, August 4, 2011

Vox, There Are 28 Million Uninsured Under Obamacare. Here's Who They Are, June 29, 2017

NFIB, Facts About PPACA Individual Mandate

New York Post, The Best Hope For Cutting U.S. Drug Costs, February 14, 2018

Kaiser Permanente, Average Annual Premiums For Single And Family Coverage

Washington Examiner, Report: Nearly all, 99.8%, of illegal drugs shipped to U.S. from Mexico, November 22, 2016

CDC, Adult Obesity Facts

Bloomberg, Why The $600 EpiPen Costs $69 In Britain, September 28, 2016

Drugs.com, FDA Approval Process

Chapter Five

Gallup, Abortion

Life News, Premature Baby Born At 21 Weeks And The Side Of A Soda Can Defies The Odds, Turns 1, July 19, 2018

Washington Post, For Planned Parenthood Abortion Stats, 3 Percent And 94 Percent Are Both Misleading, August 12, 2015

The Daily Signal, The Numbers That Show Planned PArenthood About Abortion, Not Women's Health, September 14, 2016

Chapter Six

Pew Research, U.S. Student's Academic Achievement Still Lags That Of Their Peers In Many Other Countries, February 15, 2017

PolitiFact, Does The United States Spend More Per Student Than Most Countries?, April 21, 2015

*Washington Post, How Many Ineffective Teachers Are Actually Out There?, February 19, 2013
National Center For Educational Statistics*

New York Times, Class Size Around The World, September 11, 2009

USA Today, Here's The Average American Household Income: How Do You Compare?, November 24, 2016

Infoplease, School Years Around The World

Center For Public Education, Time In School: How Does The U.S. Compare?

*The Economist, How Global University Rankings
Are Changing Higher Education, May 19, 2018*

*Federal Reserve Bank Of Minneapolis, Consumer
Price Index*

U.S. Department Of Education, Budget Summary

*Forbes, The Countries With The Most STEM
Graduates, February 2, 2017*

Wikipedia, Federal Direct Student Loan Program

Chapter Seven

*Bloomberg, Get Rid Of Capitalism? Millenials Are
Ready To Talk About It, November 6, 2017*

*Foundation For Economic Education, Capitalism Is
Good For The Poor, June 9, 2016*

*Contracting Business, Ten Reasons Why Capitalism
Is Morally Superior, September 25, 2015*

*The Daily Wire, 5 Statistics Showing How
Capitalism Solves Poverty, March 18, 2017*

*Townhall, 5 Ways Socialism Destroys Societies,
February 25, 2014*

Forbes, Socialism Is Bad, February 12, 2017

*The Epoch Times, Is Central Banking A Capitalist
Or Communist Concept?, February 9, 2017*

*New York Times, Venezuela Inflation Could Reach
One Million Percent By Year's End, July 23, 2018*

The Hill, Tariffs Are Bad Policy, April 24, 2018

Chapter Eight

National Interest, Should The U.S. LEave NATO, December 7, 2015

Office Of The Historian, North Atlantic Treaty Organization

The Hill, Who Needs NATO, July 9, 2018

New York Times, Time For The U.S. To Leave NATO, September 16, 2013

CNN Money, These NATO Countries Are Not Paying Their Fair Share On Defense, July 8, 2016

Gallup, United Nations

Business Insider, The World's 20 Strongest Militaries, October 3, 2015

Firstpost, Get This: World Owes U.S. Nearly As Much As It Owes World, September 1, 2011

Chapter Nine

Cornell Law School, First Amendment

*Washington Post, Supreme Court Unanimously
Reaffirms: There Is No "Hate Speech" Exception
To The First Amendment, June 19, 2017*

*ABC News, One Dead, At Least 30 Injured After
Violent Clashes, Car Ramming In Charlottesville*

Justia, U.S. Supreme Court, Houchins V. KQED Inc

Plaza, Landmark Libel Cases

Wikipedia, United States Defamation Law

Chapter Ten

*Forbes, How American Citizens Finance $18.5
Billion In Healthcare For Unauthorized
Immigrants, February 26, 2018*

*Wikipedia, Economic Impact Of Illegal Immigrants
In The United States*

*Federation For American Immigration Reform, The
Fiscal burden Of Illegal Immigration On United
States Taxpayers*

Brookings, The Wall, August 2017

*ABC News, Obama Has Deported More People
Than Any Other President, August 29, 2016*

*Pew Research Center, Sesame Street Reaches Out
To 2.7 Million American Children With An
Incarcerated Parent, June 21, 2013*

Wikipedia, Immigration To The United States

INDEX

A

F

However, 8-10

I

If, 5, 10
if, 6-8
immediately, 9
immensely, 6
Immigration, 4
impact, 9-10
importantly, 5
improves, 6
in, 5-10
income, 6-10
increase, 6-10
increased, 7-8, 10
indeed, 5
Index, 4
individual, 6-7
individuals, 9
into, 6, 9
introduced, 5
investment, 9
investors, 8
is, 5-10
isn, 8
It, 5
it, 5, 7, 9-10

its, 5

J

jobs, 10
Jr, 5
Just, 7

K

Kennedy, 7
King, 5

L

laffer, 7
large, 5
larger, 5
largest, 5
lead, 2
leading, 10
less, 6
level, 8
Liberalism, 2
Liberties, 4
life, 10
like, 5
little, 5
living, 10
losing, 8
loss, 6, 8-10

my, 3

N

nation, 10
needs, 5-6
neither, 5
net, 10
New, 8
new, 8, 10
next, 6
no, 5-6
nor, 5
not, 5-7, 9
now, 5
number, 8

O

obese, 10
obesity, 10
obviously, 6
occur, 9
of, 5-10
Office, 8
offset, 5, 10
On, 5, 9
on, 5-10
once, 10